Growing up in
PURITAN TIMES

Amanda Clarke

B. T. Batsford Ltd *London*

ISBN 0 7134 3366 3

Printed by The Garden City Press, Letchworth, Herts.
for the Publishers B T Batsford Limited
4 Fitzhardinge Street, London W1H 0AH

Frontispiece: **Richard Cromwell**

Acknowledgment

The Author and Publishers thank the following
for their kind permission to reproduce copyright
illustrations: BBC Hulton Picture Library for
frontispiece and figs 2, 3, 4, 6, 7, 9, 17, 21, 25,
26, 32, 33, 37, 40, 44, 47, 59; The Trustees of the
British Museum for fig 50; Dover Publications for
fig 11 (from Pat Hodgson Library); Mary Evans
Picture Library for figs 27, 63; General Post Office
for fig 52 (by courtesy of H.M. Postmaster-General);
Pat Hodgson Library for fig 61; Mansell Collection
for figs 5, 8, 12, 15, 16, 31, 38, 39, 41, 42, 43,
46, 51, 55, 58, 62; Peter Newark's Historical Pictures
for figs 1, 13, 14, 18, 22, 23, 24, 28, 30, 34, 35,
36, 48, 53, 54, 56, 57, 60; Tate Gallery, London
for fig 19; Victoria and Albert Museum for figs 10,
49. Thanks are expressed also to Pat Hodgson for
the picture research on the book.

Contents

The Illustrations

1 The Puritan Age

1 The state seal of Oliver Cromwell. Cromwell chose to put the map of England and Ireland on the seal, instead of his own portrait. England was at war with Scotland, therefore Scotland was left off the map. The English fleet had control of the English Channel.

Strictly speaking, the Puritan Age in England lasted from 1649 to 1660. This was the period after the Civil Wars and the execution of King Charles I, in which England was governed as a republic under Oliver Cromwell

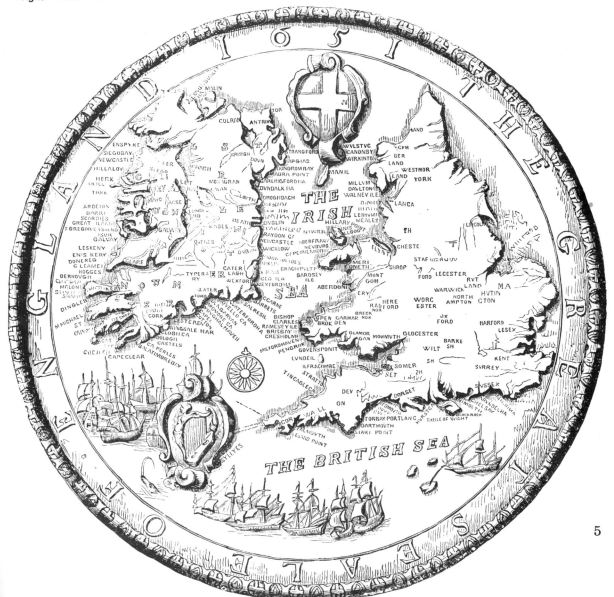

THE BRITISH SEA

2 Oliver Cromwell, Lord Protector of England, 1653-58.

3 Richard Cromwell became Lord Protector at ➤ his father's death in 1658, but abdicated in 1659.

(until 1658) and his son, Richard (1658-60). This eleven-year period is known as the Interregnum, or as the Commonwealth (because England was named "a Commonwealth or Free State"), or as the Protectorate (after Cromwell had become Lord Protector in 1653). The existence of the Republic relied entirely on the personality of Cromwell, with the assistance of the Army, and it collapsed shortly after his death.

However, although the Puritan Age is strictly 1649 to 1660, the Puritans had been in virtual power since the early 1640s, and a group of people called Puritans had been recognized since the reign of Elizabeth I (1558-1603).

Who were the Puritans?

When Elizabeth I came to the throne in 1558, an Act of Parliament declared that from then on the official religion of England was to be Protestantism. The Church of England was the Established Church of England. The Queen became the Supreme Governor of the Church, an Act of Uniformity was passed, a Common Prayer Book was introduced and Thirty-Nine Articles were drawn up which all clergy had to accept. This Elizabethan church settlement was a mixture of Catholic and Protestant elements and most people were happy with it. However, some thought that it was too moderate and that it did not contain enough reforms. They were anxious to eliminate all remaining traces of Catholicism from the Church of England. Gradually a group of such people emerged, who were nicknamed Puritans, because they wanted to *purify* the Church. A lady called Lucy Hutchinson described them as "the more religious zealots who afterwards were branded with the name Puritans". The nickname did not greatly please them, as one man complained in 1580:

> very cunningly hath men christened us with an odious name, of Puritanism. We detest both the name and the heresy.

He considered that to be called a Puritan was little better than being called a "bloodsucker".

At first the Puritans were a minority group, but by the end of the sixteenth century, in spite of government opposition and persecution, the party had gathered strength and influence. To call the Puritans a party is perhaps misleading, for the Puritans were by no means united in ideas or beliefs. Many were moderates who simply wanted reforms within the Church of England. For example, they objected to the length and fussiness of the church services; the use of the cross at baptisms; the use of a ring at marriages; the surplices worn by the priests.

7

4 Puritans avidly reading the Bible. They believed that every individual should be able to interpret the Scriptures for himself.

They wanted a much simpler service in which the sermon was the most important part. They stressed that each individual Christian should be allowed to interpret the Bible in his own way.

More extreme Puritans were so discontented with the Established Church that instead of going to church services, they worshipped secretly in their own homes, with a Puritan priest. This group became known as Separatists, because they wanted to separate themselves from the Church of England. They disliked the authority of the Bishops, who they thought had too much wealth and power. They believed in Pre-Destination: which means that they thought that everyone, before birth, had been elected either to go to Heaven or to go to Hell, and that nothing could alter this.

5 A satirical drawing of a Scottish Presbyterian on a set of playing cards.

A third group of Puritans, later called the Independents, wanted a decentralized church, with power in the hands of each individual congregation, rather than with the Bishop in charge of the whole region. And other sects developed, including the Quakers, Baptists and Fifth Monarchy Men, all with their particular brand of Puritanism.

The Puritans and James I

When James I came to the throne in 1603, many Puritans thought that he would be sympathetic to their demands for reform, since he had had a Presbyterian upbringing. He did allow some reforms of the Book of Common Prayer, but he would not agree to give more power to the local clergy instead

6 A Puritan family group in Holland. Puritans from England emigrated to Holland, where the Protestant church was more simple and strict as they preferred. However, they found life in Holland very strange.

of letting the Bishops decide on issues. "No Bishop, no King," he said — to take away the power of the Bishops would be like leaving the country with no king.

Some Puritans then emigrated to Holland, which had long supported the more rigid forms of Protestantism. When in 1620 it was feared that Holland would be overrun by Spain, which was staunchly Catholic, a group of Puritans, who now called themselves Pilgrims, decided to try to settle in North America. In July they sailed from Delft Haven in Holland, in a ship called the *Speedwell*, to Southampton and here another boat of Pilgrims, the *Mayflower* was ready to sail with them. Three hundred miles off the coast of England the *Speedwell* sprung a leak and all the 120 pilgrims eventually had to travel in the *Mayflower*. The Pilgrim Fathers founded a colony in Virginia. More

Puritan families joined them and that area, known as New England, became a Puritan land. Life there was described in a ballad called "The Zealous Puritan":

> *There you may teach our hymns*
> *Without the laws controulment;*
> *We need not fear the Bishops there,*
> *Nor spiritual courts involvement;*
> *Nay, the surplice shall not fright us,*
> *Nor superstition blind us.*

The Puritans and Charles I

By the time Charles I became King in 1625, Puritans were dominant in the House of Commons. Charles I, however, seemed more friendly towards the Catholics. He selected William Laud as Archbishop of Canterbury, who strongly opposed the Puritans. Puritanism became a political as well as a religious issue, because by stating that they were anti the Established Church, of which

7 Puritans on their way to church in New England, America. In the new land they were free to worship as they believed right.

M.ͬ Henry Burton, for preaching againſt Po
piſh innovations and printing his 2 Sermons
For God & the king, was much vexed in the high,
Commiſſion Court, afterward cenſured in the
Starr-Chamber to be deprived of his Miniſtrie,
degraded in the Vniverſty, loſt both his Eares on
the pillorie, was fined 5000,͓ baniſhed into the Ile
of Gernſey, there Comͤitted to perpetuall cloſs im
priſonment, where no freinds, no not ſo much
as his wife or Children, might once ſee or come
into the Iſland where hee was on pain of im,
priſonment to them, Which Corporall puniſh:
ment was Executed on him, and his two other bleſſed
Brethren or fellow-Sufferers, June 30.ͭʰ 1637,

8　Puritans, such as Mr Henry Burton, died for their beliefs during the reign of Charles I who favoured Catholic ideas. The punishments Henry Burton suffered for criticizing Catholic ways are listed here.

9　Oliver Cromwell soon stood out as the leading figure in the Parliament after the execution of Charles I, but he refused to become King of England. This painting is of Cromwell refusing the crown.

Charles I was the head, they were also saying that they were against the King as head of the State. The conflict between Charles I and his Parliament led to the Civil Wars of 1642-49, in which the country ranged itself on the side of the Royalists (supporters of the King and the Established Church) or the Parliamentarians (supporters of Parliament and the Puritans).

Oliver Cromwell

At the end of the Civil Wars Charles I was tried and executed. The monarchy, the House of Lords and the Bishops were all abolished. Oliver Cromwell emerged as the leading figure of the new republic. He was a staunch Independent and in 1653 he introduced a Presbyterian system of Church government, with power and authority in the hands of the congregations and elders.

The Puritan rule

During the Interregnum (1649-60) almost every aspect of life was influenced by Puritanism. Puritans regarded everyone as a potential sinner and thought that the only way to Heaven was by worship of God, and hard work. They based their social standards on a literal interpretation of the

13

Scriptures. Through a series of restrictive laws, they tried to enforce a strict moral code on the life of everyone in England. For example, rigid Sunday observance was introduced, holy-days were stopped, the theatre was banned, and clothing and food and home equipment had to be simple and unextravagant.

Everyone was expected to conform to Puritan views concerning religion, although Cromwell was surprisingly tolerant of the Catholics. He did not introduce any new laws against them, nor did he rigorously enforce the old ones. However, celebration of mass was forbidden, so that Catholics and High Anglicans had to either worship in secret or go abroad. Many people did worship in private, while outwardly conforming to Puritanism. Masses were held in private chapels of foreign embassies in London, for example. Jews were allowed to return to the country for the first time in several hundred years. But, on the whole, the Puritans did enforce their religious beliefs very harshly.

In spite of the restrictive laws, much did flourish during the Puritan Age. Cromwell was successful in foreign policy and the foundations of the future British Empire were laid. In 1654 naval supremacy was established in the West Indies and Jamaica was captured, although few families were willing to emigrate there. The Treaty of Westminster in the same year gave England undisputed control in the Channel. Her nearest rival, Holland, agreed to honour the English flag and not to give help to Royalists. Treaties with countries such as Sweden, Denmark and Portugal helped to boost trade.

It was a time of great interest in education. Milton, for example, wanted to establish academies all over the country, which would give a complete and general education for boys between the ages of twelve and twenty-one. He also thought that every village should have a schoolmaster, who

10   A miniature painted by Samuel Cooper, in about 1653.

would teach idle children and prevent them from becoming thieves or beggars. A petition in 1641 demanded that, in addition to Oxford and Cambridge, a third university should be set up in the north of England, and a college was founded in Durham. Unfortunately, it was destroyed at the Restoration.

The Arts did not suffer by the Puritans' restrictions on entertainment as much as is often assumed. Samuel Cooper, believed by some to be the best English painter of miniatures, was producing much work during this period, including portraits of Cromwell. Although theatres were banned, the first English opera dates from the Commonwealth. Puritans enjoyed music, providing it was not "effeminate and lust provoking", and John Player, the first regular music publisher in England, printed two works at this time — *The English Dancing Master* in 1650 and *A Brief Introduction to the Skill of Musick* in 1654. As for literature, vast numbers of pamphlets and sermons were published. John Milton was the major Puritan writer. He was one of the more extreme Puritans, and wanted to "justify the ways of God to man".

Strict and austere as the Puritans were,

they were not above criticism. Lucy Hutchinson disgustedly described Cromwell's court as being "full of sin and vanity, and the more abominable because they had not quite cast away the name of God, but profaned it by taking it in vain". However, in the end, too much restriction and too little pleasure turned many families away from Puritanism and the Restoration of King Charles II in 1660 was warmly received with the cry of "let religion alone, give me my small liberty".

11　A page from a pamphlet against money-lending, published in 1634. The usurer is likened to a greedy pig.

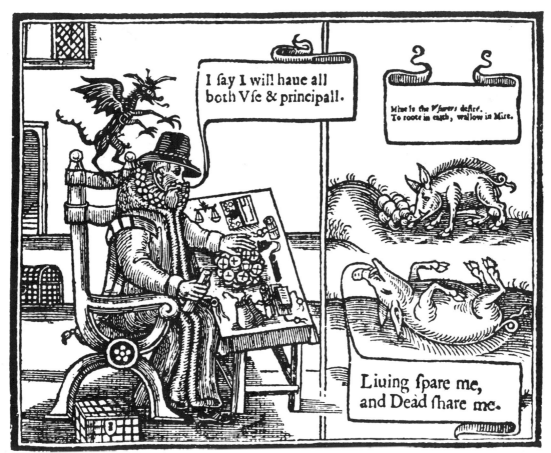

2 The Family

The average size of a family in Puritan times was 4.5 people, excluding the servants and apprentices who might also live in the house. The birth rate was high, but it was expected that many of the children born would not survive to adulthood. Indeed, only one out of five babies who survived birth was expected to reach its first birthday. The high infant mortality rate was due to lack of medical knowledge and to general insanitary conditions. However, there were some large families. In 1653 a lady named Dame Hester Temple and her children "had so exceedingly multiplied that this lady saw 700 extracted from her body". But she was the exception rather than the rule. Surprisingly, many illegitimate children were born during Puritan times. The unfortunate mother received a severe scolding, or even a public whipping.

Puritan parents

The Puritans considered the family unit very important. The father was unquestionably the head of the Puritan family. He was "master of the house" and "by the right of nature, hath principality and sovereignty therein". His word was law, and he was strict and authoritarian. His children addressed him as "sir" and had to kneel or stand in his presence, the boys first removing their hats. Apparently, not all fathers were sympathetic towards their children, for one complained:

> what a deal of patience is requisite to bear any converse with our little children.

How peevish and foolish they are.

The mother was addressed as "madam" and also demanded respect and politeness from her children. She was expected to be a paragon of virtue and skills. Gervase Markham in his book *The English Housewife* gave a list of the "inward and outward virtues, which ought to make a complete woman".

12   The Duke and Duchess of Newcastle and their family, 1656. ►

13   Oliver Cromwell's wife. She wears white falling bands (collars).
▼

These included:

skill in Physick, surgery, cookery, extraction of oils, banqueting stuff, ordering of great feasts, preserving of all sorts of wines, conceited secrets, distillations of perfumes, ordering of wool, hemp or flax; making cloth and dyeing, the knowledge of dairies, the office of malting, of oats, their exellent uses in family brewing, baking and all things belonging to a household.

Not all Puritan mothers approved of the brewing part of household management, for the Puritans considered that intoxicating beverages were sinful. Advice was handed down from mother to daughter on

14 This picture of an early Puritan family in 1563 illustrates how children were instructed in religious knowledge by their father. The father is teaching his family the Psalms.

15 A painting by F.D. Millet, an American artist of the nineteenth century, called "The Black Sheep". The father of the Puritan family reproaches the girl for bad behaviour.

how to best run a household and bring up a family. Everything had to be done by hand. The Puritans tried to correct extravagance and luxury, and so a Puritan mother was expected to be thrifty and economical in her management, and to encourage a plain and simple way of living.

Children

Puritans believed that children were essentially bad, but that they could be saved from the flames of Hell if they were brought up strictly and religiously. Children were expected to behave politely and modestly at all times, and to respect their elders. To do anything that would bring shame or embarrassment on the family was considered shocking. One man remarked:

> Let an 100 vagabonds . . . play the filthy persons . . . this brings no discredit to the father . . . but if his son . . . shall do any such things, himself hath not the blot alone, but he bringeth also an evil report upon the family.

Extreme Puritan parents gave their children unusual and sometimes absurd names. The names which Ben Jonson gave to the characters in *Bartholomew Fair* were meant to be funny, but they could well have been chosen by Puritans. For example, there were people called Zeal of the Land Busy and Mistress Win the Fight Littlewit! These names were made up, but a member of one of Cromwell's Parliaments was actually called Obadiah Praise be to God Barebones! Less zealous parents named their girl children Faith, Patience, Hope or Ruth, for example, and their boys Joshua, Abraham or Joseph. Many names were picked at random from the Bible. Other less fortunate children were labelled with terrible names such as Lament, Helpless and Sorry for Sin.

Birth

Mothers always had their babies at home, usually helped by some close friends and a midwife. Childbirth was a difficult, dangerous time, and mothers and babies frequently died. A baby's birth was registered in the parish records, but the Puritans frowned on and, after 1650, did not allow the traditional baptism ceremony or the celebrations that had followed it.

Marriage

Puritan children lived at home until they were married, unless they were apprenticed to learn a craft. Girls could marry when they were twelve, and boys when they were fourteen, but the average age for marriage seems to have been the early twenties. Children were expected to marry according to the wishes of their parents, who were shocked if a marriage took place without their approval. Girls were expected to bring a useful dowry of money or land to their future husband.

Puritans believed that a wedding should be as simple as possible, without the lavish parties and celebrations that had accompanied weddings in the past. From 1652 civil marriages were compulsory. In other words, the couple had to be married by a magistrate rather than a priest. This changed the whole character of weddings. The Prayer Book was no longer used. Instead, the service was conducted from the Puritan Directory, and the couple merely had to swear before two witnesses. The exchanging of rings was also abolished. Here is how Anne Murray, a Royalist, described her wedding in 1656. The ending is interesting.

> The Justice performed what was usual for him at that time, which was only holding up ye Directory in his hand, asked Sir James if he intended to marry me; and asked if I intended to marry him. I said yes. Then says he "I pronounce you man and wife" so calling for a glass of

The Portraiture of Mr Praise God Barebone

sack, he drunk and wished much happiness to us; and we left him, having given his clerk money, who gave [us] a parchment, the day and witness and attested by the Justice that he had married us. But had it not been done more solemnly afterwards by a minister I should not have believed it lawfully done.

Once married, the couple were expected to stay together for life, and the wife was expected to obey her husband in everything. Separation was known, but was much frowned upon. There were no Divorce Courts, but the idea was mentioned. Milton was one of the first people to bring up the idea.

Death

Life expectancy was much shorter than it is now, and not many people lived to see their fiftieth birthday. This and the high mortality rate of children meant that death was a frequent and familiar occurrence and it was therefore less feared than today. For Puritans, death was a time of reckoning, when the dead person was punished or rewarded according to his or her behaviour on earth. The Puritans disapproved of traditional funerals, which had wakes and elaborate mourning rituals. Instead, their ceremonies were simple, and there was civil registration of the death. Sometimes rings were especially made to commemorate the dead person. They often had his or her initials on them. The rings were given to the closest relatives.

◄ **16** Mr Praise be to God Barebones, **member of parliament. Extreme Puritans gave their children religiously significant names like this.**

17 Oliver Cromwell lying in state, **not in a church, but in Somerset House. The Puritans were against any elaborate church ceremonies, including for funerals.**

▼

3 Home Life

The Puritans thought that following fashion — be it in clothing or architecture or whatever — was frivolous and unnecessary. Only the bare essentials were permitted in a life devoted to the worship of God. Austerity and simplicity were therefore the keys to Puritan home life.

Clothing

In the early seventeenth century, when the fashion in dress had been for bright colours, elaborate styles and masses of lace and ribbons, the Puritans had been conspicuous by their dull, dark clothing, with no lace or trimmings. During the Commonwealth (1649-60) most Puritan families wore modified versions of the old Royalist clothes, but were urged to give up the "trimmings of lace, ribbons and useless buttons . . . by mistake called ornament".

Babies' clothing

A new-born baby was wrapped in swaddling bands in which it remained cocooned for up to four months. A long strip of cloth, six inches wide and ten feet long, was tightly wound around the baby's body. This practice had been going on for hundreds of years, and like everyone else, Puritan mothers believed that the swaddling bands would keep the baby out of mischief and make its limbs grow straight. On top of the swaddling bands, babies wore layers of other clothes. They had nightcaps called "biggins", bibs and even soft corsets, called "stay-bands". The beautiful clothes of former generations were frowned upon by the Puritans, who did not allow their babies any lacy creations. Babies slept in wooden cradles and had rattles and teething rings. Infants learnt to walk with the help of special leading reins, called hanging sleeves, attached to their clothes.

18 Dress in 1657. The drawing was made from the tomb of Hyacinth and Elizabeth Sacheverel.

19 The baby of a rich family, tightly swaddled and well wrapped in further layers of clothing.

Children's clothing

Children were expected to be neat, with their hair always tidy, their shoes shining and their clothes clean. They wore smaller versions of their parents' clothes. Girls wore long skirts and separate bodices, with large, plain white collars (falling bands) and cuffs, and a white apron. Hair was neatly coiled or kept hidden under a little cap.

Little boys wore the same long skirts as their sisters, until they were formally "breeched" sometime between their fourth and sixth birthdays. Boys then wore breeches, jerkins and doublets, with large collars and white cuffs. Only the more extreme sort of Puritan wore one of the large black hats which are frequently seen in films or illustrations to story-books about Puritans.

20 Puritan girl's dress. ➤

Here are some of the items in one boy's wardrobe in the 1650s:

two mantles [cloaks] . . . one of them scarlet bound by red binding with gold and silver on it, of three finger broad; the other mantle was of grey serge, bound with a blue binding, and a silver lace on it . . . one pair of green lace stockings, one cloak, an riding coat, two doublets, and one pair of breeches of beaver grey cloth.

This boy was obviously not from an extreme Puritan family.

Girls

Some young people obviously did follow fashion still. In 1650 an extreme Puritan called John Bulwer was disgusted by the way young girls were wearing corsets to

21 Oliver Cromwell and his son. The boy wears a smaller version of his father's clothes.

give themselves the slender waists they thought fashionable. By this "deadly artifice", he said

> they reduce their breasts into such straights that they soon purchase a stinking breath . . . and to that end by strong compulsion shut up their waists in a whalebone prison of little ease,

they open a door to consumptions, and a withering rottenness.

On the other hand, many Puritans thought corsets a good thing for they disciplined the body.

An Act was passed in 1650 to stop girls wearing make-up or beauty spots, and "immodest dress". It does not seem to have been very effective, for in May 1654 even a Royalist, John Evelyn was surprised to note that "the women began to paint themselves, formerly a most ignominious thing and used only by prostitutes".

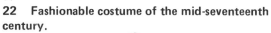

▲
22   Fashionable costume of the mid-seventeenth century.

▲
23   Ladies wore patches on their faces, in spite of a law passed in 1650 banning the wearing of make-up or beauty spots.

Boys

The fashion for boys, according to one older Puritan, was to have

> half shirts and half arms . . . they must have narrow waists, and narrow bands [collars], large cuffs upon their wrists and larger upon their shin bones; their boots must be crimped, and their knees guarded . . . a man would [think] them apes by their coats, soap-makers by their faces, meal men by their shoulders, bears or dogs by their frizzled hair . . .

Boys were supposed to wear their hair cropped, but many preferred more elaborate styles or even to experiment with wigs.

24 An extreme fashion follower of 1646. The Puritans spoke strongly against such extravagance. Notice the long hair, the patches on the man's face, and the wide cuffs round his shins.

"These periwigs of false coloured hair are utterly unlawful and condemned by Christ himself", declared one horrified Puritan. And another said that

> our patched faces are enough to make us monsters in God's eyes . . . our powdered hair to fetch God's razor to shave these besmeared looks.

However, it seems that even good Puritans could be criticized for their hair styles: they wore their hair

> long enough to cover their ears, and the ministers and many others cut it close around their heads, with so many little peaks, as it was something ridiculous to behold.

Homes

Houses were plainly furnished, and equipped only with the essentials, although some families did employ servants to do the cleaning and cooking. Tapestries hung on the walls, and the floors were bare, highly polished boards. Curtains were rare and usually used only as draught-excluders over doors. Furniture was made of wood, but was slightly less heavy than in Jacobean and Elizabethan times. People sat on benches and stools, although the father might have a chair. Tables and sideboards, cupboards and chests were familiar articles in every home. The largest and most valuable piece of furniture was the four-poster bed. Of course, Puritan beds had far less ornate bed hangings than previous generations.

Hygiene

More care was taken over cleanliness than in the past, but Puritan families were more concerned about the cleanliness of the mind than that of the body. Washing meant a quick dip in cold water every morning. Few homes had bathrooms. A wooden tub was put in front of the fire and filled with water, when a bath was required. Some towns did have public baths, including Turkish ones, but they were not considered "nice" places to go to. Toothbrushes were known by this period, but were not widely used. Most people rubbed their teeth with a piece of cloth, or used a toothpick.

25 Furniture of the mid-seventeenth century, ▶ set out in the Stuart Room of the Geffrye Museum.

Lavatories had been introduced in 1597, but few houses had them installed. Instead, the close-stool was used. This was a padded box with a chamber-pot mounted inside. It had a lid and handles so that it could be carried around the house. Chamber-pots were most commonly used, and were made of everything from earthenware to pewter.

Cleaning the house and doing the family washing were major chores which were not undertaken very often. One way to clean soiled linen which was recommended to Puritan mothers was to soak it in a mixture of water and sheep's dung for two days; then wring it out and put a mixture of dog's mercury, mallow and wormwood (plants) all over it; then pour boiling water over it, and leave it to stand for a day. The whole process then had to be repeated, after which the linen was meant to be spotless! No wonder washing was done only every two months or so!

Sickness

No one suspected that dirt might be the cause of the illness and disease which were common. Remedies for various illnesses were a mixture of magic and tradition, and cannot have been very effective. Natural horse dung was supposed to sooth burns, but if fried first, it was good for bruises. If someone had been bitten by an adder, a compound of hazel nuts, rue and garlic mashed with treacle would help. With cures such as these, it is not surprising that even the most common and apparently harmless illness could be fatal. One poor man fractured his ankle, but it was so badly set that it festered and eventually had to be amputated. Unfortunately, the amputation was also bungled so that in the end he died.

Rickets was one of the most common of children's illnesses. It was probably caused by a lack of calcium in their diet, and one of

The true and liuely Pourtraicture of Valentine Greatrakes Esq
of Affane in y County of Waterford in y Kingdome of Ireland
famous for curing several Deseases and distempers
by the stroak of his Hand only.

the main symptoms was a general crooked-ness of the limbs. (This was one of the things which swaddling hoped to prevent.) A boy suffering from rickets was described by his mother:

For Jack, his legs are most miserable crooked as ever I saw any child's, and yet thank God he goes strongly and is very straight in his body as any child can be.

One remedy was to put children into leather corsets, another to make them eat raven's liver. Between 1658 and 1660 fifteen thousand children were suffering from rickets.

Other illnesses included smallpox, typhoid and measles, but the most feared was the plague. One disgusting "cure" for plague was to cut up four ounces of dried human flesh, add it to wine and then set it in horse dung for a month — by which time the sufferer must have died anyway! To prevent catching the plague, a medicine was made up out of the brains of a young man who had died a violent death, mixed with the nerves, arteries and pith of the backbone. This medicine was left to ferment for six months, after which time a drop a day guaranteed immunity.

Food and drink

Puritan families strongly disapproved of gluttony and had simple fare for their meals. Cromwell's wife recommended a simple diet, saying that "the Kingdom of God is not meat and drink but righteous-ness and peace". Not many people agreed with her and they laughed at her boast that she gave her husband marrow pudding for breakfast and hog's liver and sausages for his dinner. She must have made an exception for her Gooseberry Cream, which is a very rich recipe:

first boil or you may preserve your gooseberries, then a clear cream boiled up and seasoned with cinnamon, nutmeg, mace, sugar, rose water and eggs; dish it up and when it is cold, take up the goose-berries with a pin and stick them in on rounds as thick as they can lie upon the said cream, garnishing your dish with them, and strew them over with the finest sugar and serve them up.

There were three meals a day, and a prayer was said before and after each one. Break-fast was served at 6.00 a.m. and consisted of porridge, bread and cheese. The main meal of the day was taken at midday, when soup, meats, vegetable stews and custards were available. Supper was a light meal served between 5.00 and 8.00 p.m. Children were expected to serve their parents first, and to remain seated at the table until they had permission to leave.

Meat was eaten in large quantities and included venison, beef, mutton, chicken and brawn. Vegetables were regarded with a certain amount of suspicion, and were believed to cause wind. Although a huge variety were available, including parsnips, beans, artichokes, spinach and cabbage, they were rarely eaten on their own but made into stews. Fruit was also plentiful and two new fruits were introduced during the Commonwealth — bananas and pine-apples. Bananas were not eaten raw but were made into dumplings and tarts. Pine-apples were considered to be "dangerous" and were looked on as a curiosity rather than food. Sweet things were popular, including syllabubs and custards. It was believed that

That which preserveth apples and plums
Will also preserve liver and lung.

Food was cooked on open fires or hearths, and could be boiled, baked or stewed. Bread and pies were baked in a brick oven, a useful thing which most homes had. Sometimes Puritan mothers saved fuel by cooking together. Knives and spoons were the main items of cutlery, but forks were just becoming popular. Sometimes knives were converted into forks by shortening the blade and splitting it down the middle. Three-pronged forks were not known for another twenty years.

27 A dog-wheel was used to turn the spit over the fire in this seventeenth-century kitchen. The dog inside the wheel walked it round, so turning the spit.

All alcoholic drink was considered sinful, but ale remained the most popular drink, enjoyed by everyone including children. Coffee, tea and chocolate had been introduced to England, but were luxuries and therefore avoided by strict Puritans.

30

4 Family Worship

28 This Puritan satire from the reign of Charles I shows on the left a Puritan ("Of God"), in the middle Archbishop Laud, and on the right a court Bishop. The Puritan holds the English Bible, the Archbishop has the Service Book and the Bishop has a Latin book. The Puritans and the Bishops were great enemies, and as soon as the Puritans came to power in 1649 the Bishops were abolished.

During the few years in which the Puritans were in power the structure of the Church of England and people's attitudes towards religious worship changed enormously. The Bishops had been abolished and the Presbyterian system of church government by elders and congregations was introduced in 1653.

▲
29   In 1643 the Puritans tore down the cross in Cheapside, London. They did not like extravagant religious symbols.

30   The Puritans replaced the church bell with ➤ a drum.

The Puritans believed that the purpose of life was to serve God, and that worship of God should be as pure and free from popery as possible. To achieve this purity of worship, churches and services had to be plain and unadorned. Therefore "steeple-houses" — which was the Puritan's nickname for churches — were stripped of their finery, which included ancient statues of saints, beautiful stained glass windows and decorated altars. The services were shortened and considerably altered. The Book of Common Prayer was replaced by the Puritan Directory, which set down shorter services with emphasis on the sermon; and after 1650, traditional ceremonies such as baptisms, weddings and funerals were disallowed and replaced

with civil registrations. All religious festivals and holy-days were banned, and strict observance of the Sabbath (Sabbatarianism) held the country in a vice-like grip.

The family
The Puritans believed that love of God began in the home:

If ever we would have the Church of God to continue among us we must bring it into our households and nourish it in our families.

They thought that it was the duty of the father to make sure that his family worshipped regularly and led true Christian

32

lives. Fathers were advised to

first reform your families and then you will be fitter to reform the family of God. Let the master reform the servant, the father the child, the husband his wife.

In 1648 it was decided that to neglect family prayer was a sin. Therefore, the Puritan family spent many hours every day in private worship, as well as going to church on Sunday. Prayers were held two or three times a day, not counting those said before and after meals. In an attempt to make his family a "little church", as was desirable, the father led Bible readings, and taught his children and servants the catechism. Every

Puritan child was familiar with the Bible and was expected to learn large chunks of it by heart. On Sundays the clergyman often dropped in to talk to the children on some religious topic. Sometimes the father ordered his family to go on a fast for a day, and no one was allowed to eat or drink. Sometimes, if an epidemic was threatening, which was seen as a punishment from God, the whole country fasted as a means of asking for God's forgiveness. In November 1655 the town of Coventry fasted in an attempt to be saved from an outbreak of smallpox.

31 A nineteenth-century drawing of a Puritan preaching a sermon.

Church going

Churches were locked on weekdays, but on Sundays everyone was expected to attend at least once. The service was conducted as laid down in the Puritan Directory, with the sermon the focal point. Even tiny babies were taken to hear the sermons, which were expected to be awe-inspiring, long-winded and passionate. One minister was fined for being too repetitive and dull. Small children were expected to be able to discuss what they had heard once they returned home, while older children took notes, using a form of shorthand. Sir Ralph Verney was not sure that this was a good idea, especially when it applied to girls: "The pride of taking sermon notes hath made multitudes of women most unfortunate." It is not absolutely clear what he meant, but it sounds as if the girls took less interest in what they heard than

32 The First Sunday in New Haven. Newly arrived in America, the Pilgrim Fathers gathered to hear a sermon.

they did in seeing how accurately and speedily they could take notes.

Fathers bought books of sermons which seem to have formed a large part of the family library.

It sounds as if the congregations were most attentive at the services, but one Frenchman was a little amazed by the things that went on in English churches in 1659:

Form they observe none . . . they pray and read without method . . . . I have beheld a whole congregation sit on their_____ with their hats on at the reading of the psalm, and yet bareheaded when they sing. In divers places they read not the

33   A Quaker is whipped by the hangman to the
Old Exchange, London, 1656.

34   A spell in the stocks was another punishment ➤
for not attending a church service in Puritan times.

Scriptures at all, but up into the pulpit, where they make an insipid tedious and unmethodical prayer, and a tone so affected and mysterious that they give it the name of canting, after which there follows a sermon . . . consisting of speculative and abstracted notions, and things which nor the people nor themselves well understand; but they extend to extraordinary lengths . . . and well they may for their chairs are lined with . . . velvet cushions upon which they loll . . . till almost they sleep.

Sunday observance

The Bible lays down that the Sabbath day is to be kept as a day of rest. The Puritans interpreted this literally and refused to allow practically any activity on a Sunday. "No worldly labour or work of ordinary calling" was permitted, which covered everything from cooking to going for a walk. Shopkeepers were not allowed to buy or sell, servants were not allowed to cook or clean, and travel of any sort was strictly forbidden, unless it was to go to church.

Sunday observance was strictly enforced by soldiers. The punishments were fines, or being put in the stocks; unless the evil-doer was under twelve years old, in which case he or she was soundly whipped. There are many records of these punishments having been carried out. One man was fined ten shillings for walking to the next village to hear a sermon; three Quakers were put in a cage for having travelled to Coventry on the Lord's Day; a girl was put in the stocks for mending her dress; while a couple of sweethearts were fined for going out for a walk.

What were people meant to do on the Sabbath? Sundays were for practising the "duties of piety and true religion, publicly and privately". Everyone had to attend a church service:

> rogues, vagabonds and beggars, do on every Sabbath day repair to some church and chapel and shall remain there soberly and orderly during the time of divine worship.

Three men loitering at an ale-house in Coventry at the time of public worship were put in the stocks. Therefore, Sundays, which were usually the only days on which people did not have to work, ceased to be a time of enjoyment and relaxation, and not everyone was pleased by it.

5 Education

In 1647 James Howell wrote

> Every man strains his fortunes to keep his children at school. The cobbler will clout till midnight, the porter will carry burdens till his bones crack again, the ploughman will pinch both back and belly to give his son learning, and I find that this ambition reigns nowhere so much as in this island.

35 A classroom in the early seventeenth century.

Why were people so anxious to keep their children at school? Religious knowledge was the most important subject taught in schools in Puritan times, and therefore many parents wanted to give their children as thorough an education as possible, so that they would gain the best grounding in Puritan beliefs. It was also thought that a good, Christian education would enable a person to work better. Therefore, education should not be confined to the privileged classes. There were many more endowed schools than in the sixteenth century, and

benefactors provided large sums of money to ensure that poor children received a sound education. However, this was not always appreciated, for the poor children who were sent to school at the expense of the benefactors would in the past have been employed and brought money into the family.

Tutors

Children of fairly wealthy parents had private tutors as soon as they were considered old enough to learn anything. This was sometimes as young as two years old, with regular lessons starting two years later. Tutors were expected to teach the basic skills of reading and writing and, of course, religious knowledge. In 1658 John Evelyn's son died at the age of five — a sad event, for his intelligence seems to have been staggering:

> At two and a half years old, he could perfectly read any of the English, Latin, French or Gothic letters, pronouncing the first three languages exactly. He had before the fifth year . . . not only the skill to read most written hands, but to decline all nouns, conjugate the verbs regular . . . turn English into Latin . . . and had a strong passion for Greek. The number of verses he could recite was prodigious . . . he had a wonderful disposition to Mathematics . . . as to his piety, astonishing as were his applications of scripture upon occasion, and his sense of God.

This little boy was exceptional, but very small children were expected to learn and perfect a large variety of subjects, many of which are not studied today.

Schools

By the middle of the seventeenth century there were approximately 1,400 schools in England and Wales, not including private ones. Only a few towns did not have at least one school, and although the schools varied in size and quality, the overall standard of teaching was high.

There were three main types of school: the petty school, the writing school and the grammar school. Children first went to either a petty school or a writing school. These were the equivalent of our primary schools. Children could enter one of these schools at any age between three and seven. Here they learnt to read and write and were given

> such preparative arts, as may make them completely fit to undergo any ordinary calling [job].

The grammar schools were open to all boys, who usually began their schooling there when they were seven and stayed at the school for eight or nine years. Some of the grammar schools accepted girls too. Some were tiny with only one room and one master, like the one at Huntingdon which Oliver Cromwell went to, while others boasted a hundred pupils and several masters and ushers (assistant teachers).

Lessons at grammar school started at 6.00 a.m. in the summer and finished at 6.00 p.m., with a two-hour break at lunchtime. In winter, the working day was shortened by an hour at each end. The main subject taught was Religious Knowledge, with emphasis on knowing the Bible. After this, the Classics were considered to be the most important. Classics consisted of Latin, Greek and Hebrew. Logic (the art of clear thinking and argument) and Rhetoric (the art of public speaking) were the other necessary subjects for a complete education. Modern subjects such as Mathematics and Science took second place, although they were encouraged in private schools. The standard varied from school to school. Frequent complaints were made against the masters, who were often brutal and made too rigorous use of the birch. One father complained that instead of being given a "true sense of learning", his son had only been taught to "construe and parse a little".

Most lessons had to be learnt by heart, for paper for writing notes was very expensive. Text-books were available, the most essential being Latin grammars and the Bible. Basic things like spellings and alphabets were printed on horn books. A horn book was a single printed page covered with a piece of transparent animal horn, which was held in place with brass clips.

Girls

A surprising number of girls were literate during this period. This was because many girls shared their brothers' tutors, and some even had their own. Most country girls went to petty schools, and some went on to grammar schools, although no girl was considered suitable for university. It was considered important for girls as well as boys, to be able to read and write, so that they could study the Bible, and handle household accounts when they were married.

Lucy Hutchinson looked back on her ability as a pupil:

By the time I was four years old I read English perfectly and having a great memory I was carried to sermons and while I was very young could remember and repeat them exactly . . . . When I was seven years of age, I remember I had at one time eight tutors in several qualities; languages, music, dancing, writing and needlework . . . . My father would learn me Latin, and I was so apt that I outstripped my brothers who were at school.

She loved to read all day long and "would never practise my lute or harpsichord but when my masters were with me; and for my needle I absolutely hated it". Not all girls received such a good education or were as able as Lucy Hutchinson, but demands were being made that there might be "places for the education of young gentlewomen". Not all fathers thought that their daughters should be learned. Sir Ralph Verney scolded his daughter for wanting to learn Latin, and told her to be content with reading her Bible.

36 Paper makers, 1659.

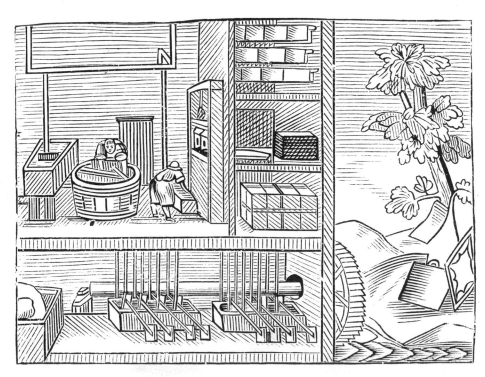

37 A horn book, with the alphabet and the Lord's Prayer.

Universities and the Inns of Court

Although the Universities had been Royalist strongholds during the Civil Wars, Puritan fathers encouraged their sons to complete their education at one of the two Universities — Oxford and Cambridge. During the Commonwealth the high standard of learning at the Universities was maintained, while the discipline was much improved. Clarendon, who was an avid Royalist, remarked that "the many who were wickedly introduced applied themselves to a study of good learning and the practice of piety". Cambridge especially appealed to Puritans. Cromwell himself had been to Sidney Sussex College there, which was once described as "a hotbed of Puritans".

Much the same subjects were taught at University as at grammar schools, but on a higher level. Religion was the prime subject, followed by the Classics, Logic and Rhetoric.

Slowly subjects such as Modern History, Philosophy, French, Italian and Mathematics were introduced. Boys usually went up to University when they were fifteen or sixteen, and stayed for four years to receive a Bachelor's degree, or seven years for a Master's degree.

Other boys went to the "third University", the nickname for the Inns of Court. Here they were trained to be lawyers. The course lasted for a minimum of seven years, although an extra ten years was considered necessary for "experience". There were four Inns of Court — Grey's Inn, Lincoln's Inn, and the Inner and Middle Temple. There were also nine smaller Inns of Chancery, where students spent a sort of probationary year. Students were expected to find their own lodgings, but the tuition was free.

38   Christ's College, Cambridge.

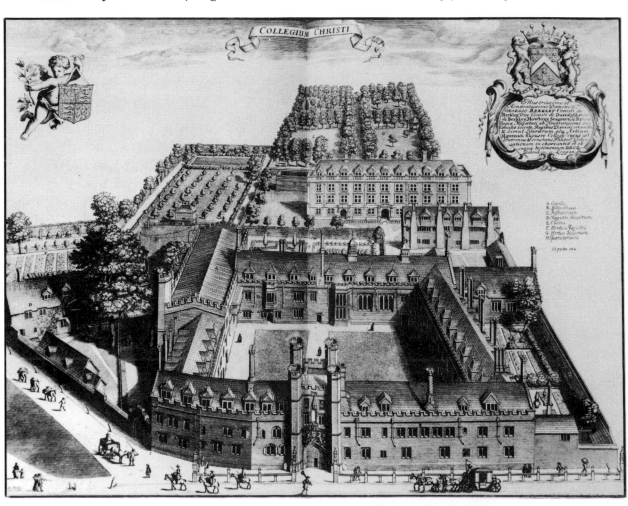

6 Amusements

We are a serious people, grim and full of cares,
And melancholy as cats, as glum as hares.

This was a traditional and fairly accurate description of Puritans. They did not spend time amusing themselves. They worked hard, believing that the Devil made work for idle hands. They thought it best to remove all possible temptations from the path of ordinary people, by banning anything that was remotely enjoyable or "sinful". Dancing round a maypole was banned and so were celebrating Christmas and the theatre. Another reason for banning entertainments like the theatre was that the Puritans were afraid that a large group of people coming together for no matter what reason might start to riot and be a threat to their authority. With no pastimes or relaxation, life must have been very dismal indeed. By 1647 people were already "hankering after the sports and pastimes they were wont to enjoy", and by 1660 most were relieved to accept the Restoration of King Charles II.

Public entertainment restricted

One of the first amusements banned by the Puritans was the theatre. Ordinances of 1642 and 1647 ordered the closure of all theatres throughout the country. The Puritans thought them to be excuses for idleness, and worst of all, that they encouraged immoral behaviour and vice. The only exception to this ban was the Red Bull in London, where "drolls", such as tight-rope-walkers and jugglers, were allowed to perform. In September 1657 John Evelyn recorded in his diary:

> Going to London . . . we stopped to see a famous rope-dancer called the Turk . . . . He walked barefooted, taking hold by his toes only of a rope almost perpendicular, and without so much as touching it with his hands; he danced blindfolded on the high rope and with a boy of twelve years old tied to one of his feet twenty foot beneath him, dangling as he danced . . . . I saw the Hairy Woman, twenty years old . . . a very large lock of hair out of each ear; she also had a most prolix beard, and moustachios, with long locks growing on the middle of her nose.

Many people protested against the closure of the theatres, especially the actors who with their wives and children were plunged into poverty. They complained that

> Other public recreations of far more harmful consequences [are] permitted still . . . namely that muse of barbarism and beastliness, the Bear Garden, whereupon . . . those demi-monsters are baited by dogs.

Bear-baiting, however, did not long outlive the theatre, and was banned along with cock-fighting in 1642.

Maypoles had been removed in 1640. Sometimes brave attempts were made to bring them back. In 1648, for example, the citizens of Bury St Edmunds "ran horribly mad upon a maypole", and in 1654 a maypole was put up in Hyde Park where "sin [was] committed by wicked meetings with fiddlers, drunkenness, ribaldry and the like".

Cromwell pypeth unto Fairfax.

39 The Puritans were against dancing and other "sinful" enjoyments. This picture from a playing card makes fun of the Puritans by showing Cromwell piping music for Fairfax, another strict Puritan, to dance to.

Holy-days restricted
Holy-days were condemned as "Devil-born heathenism" and their celebration

40 A juggler and quack doctor of London.

was strictly forbidden. But in order to give scholars, apprentices and workers the occasional day off, the Government declared that they should

have such convenient, reasonable recreation and relaxation from the constant, ordinary labours on every second Tuesday of the month throughout the year.

But there cannot have been much to do on this day of recreation.

Celebrating Christmas was banned like the other holy-days. The Puritans said that Christmas gave "liberty to carnal and sensual delights". An Act of 1644 turned Christmas Day into a fast and encouraged everyone to meditate upon their sins rather than enjoy themselves. Families were forbidden to treat Christmas Day differently from any ordinary working day, unless it fell on a Sunday, in which case the whole time was to be spent in prayer. Having a Christmas dinner was strictly not allowed and mince-

41 A drawing by a Victorian artist of a Puritan at Christmas time. The children have been caught picking holly and the man is reprimanding them for this, for the Puritans forbade any celebration of Christmas.

pies were thought to be most sinful. On one Christmas Day soldiers actually went from house to house, checking that mothers were not secretly cooking a large meal. On 25 December 1652 John Evelyn wrote in his diary: "Christmas Day, no sermon any-where, no church being permitted to be open, so observed it at home."

In 1647 the celebration of Easter was disallowed. The last Wednesday in every month was made into an official fast day, when extreme Puritan families ate nothing at all. This was to cleanse the soul. One poor boy did not think this a good idea and complained:

> not one of us, young or old, ate so much as a morsel of bread for twenty-four hours

together, which was a great weariness to me and went much against my carnal heart.

Other restrictions

In 1642 all sports and recreations such as football and dancing were forbidden. As we have seen (page 37), on a Sunday practically no activity was allowed. The time was to be spent in "reading, meditating, repetition of sermons [and] catechizing". All "fairs,

43 An organ in the seventeenth century. The man standing on the left is working the bellows.

42 Puritans burn the Book of Sports on the spot where the Cheapside Cross had stood (see picture **29**). Notice the Puritan dress of the crowd.

10 of May the Boocke of Sportes vpon the Lords day was burnt by the Hangman in the place where the Crosse stoode, & at Exhange

markets, wakes, revels, wrestlings, shootings, ringing of bells for pleasure" were banned, as were "gaming, drinking, swearing, quarrelling and other dissolute practices". In 1650 an Act was passed which laid down set fines for first-offence swearers: a Duke who swore had to pay 30 shillings, while an "inferior person" had to pay 3s. 4d. Women were fined according to the rank of their husband or father. If the offender was unable to pay the fine, he or she was put in the stocks, unless he was very young in which case he was whipped. The oaths for which swearers might be punished in these ways included "God be praised" and "Lord have mercy".

Hollar inv,
1635

Music

How did Puritan families enjoy themselves? Sermons were supposed to be a form of enjoyment, as was reading the Bible. Children no doubt continued to play favourite games such as blind-man's-buff and hide-&-seek, but probably this was only when they were well out of sight of their parents. And for people wealthy enough to afford them, hawking and hunting were still allowed, although extreme Puritans disapproved of these sports.

Music was really the only permissible form of entertainment, therefore, although there was a ban on fiddling at ale-houses and singing on the Lord's Day. Organs had been removed from churches, as they were thought to distract from the worship of God, but Milton, an extreme Puritan, had one in his own home and was very fond of playing.

◄ 44   The clavier was another popular musical instrument. The lady is not a Puritan, judging by her clothing.

Favourite musical instruments included the lute, harpsichord, viol and virginals. Many families must have enjoyed secret musical evenings, and Cromwell caused quite a stir by allowing the music of forty-eight violins and mixed dancing at the wedding of one of his daughters in 1657. Everyone enjoyed singing, whether discreetly in the home or openly in the church. Country people liked to sing ballads, which were passed down from generation to generation by the ballad-monger.

It was during the Commonwealth that the first English opera was produced. It had several public and private showings. *The Siege of Rhodes* was produced in 1656 by Sir William Davenant, who is supposed to have been the illegitimate son of Shakespeare. It was so popular, that a second opera, *The Cruelty of the Spaniards in Peru*, was written a few years later, partly as propaganda against the Spaniards and partly for pure musical pleasure.

Gardening

Another activity thought to be worthwhile was gardening. Several Puritans wrote books on the subject, such as Ralph Auster's *The Spiritual Use of an Orchard or Garden of Fruit Trees*, and Adam Speed's *Adam out of Eden*. Both authors used the Bible as a valuable source book. A gardener had to be "religious, honest and skilful" and not "a lazy lubber". Herb and kitchen gardens were very useful for medicinal and culinary purposes, and an orchard could produce grapes, plums, cherries, pears and apples. John Evelyn went to Hackney, "to see Lady Brooke's garden, which is one of the neatest and most celebrated in England", and he visited "one Mr Tomb's garden; it has large and noble walks, some modern statues, a vineyard, planted strawberry borders; staked at ten foot distances". These were probably the gardens of Royalists, rather than Puritans.

◄ 45   A ballad singer.

7 Living in a Town

Although the Puritans made some fairly drastic attempts to "purify" towns and their inhabitants, town life remained much as it always had been, except that the seamy side was concealed by a mask of Godliness. London, the capital city, was as exciting as ever. Provincial towns prospered and were colourfully described by Evelyn as he travelled round the country. He wrote of Coventry:

> the cross is remarkable . . . . This city has many handsome churches, a beautiful wall, a fair Free School and a library to it; the streets full of great shops, clean and well paved.

He judged Gloucester to be "a handsome city, considerable for the church and monuments", while Doncaster "is a large, fair town, famous for great waxlights and good stockings". Leicester he considered to be "large and pleasantly seated, but despicably built, the chimney flues like so many smiths' forges". Rutland was "pretty and well built out of stone, which [was] a rarity in this part of England, where most rural parishes are but of mud, and the people living as wretchedly as in the most impoverished parts of France". Although he admired the University buildings of Cambridge, he thought the town was "a low, dirty, unpleasant place, the streets ill-paved, the air thick and infected by the Fens". Colchester was famous for its "oysters and eringo root, growing hereabouts, and candied for sale". (Eringo was a plant whose long white roots were supposed to cure dropsy, jaundice and cholic among other diseases.)

Most towns were still rural, with many open spaces, fields and gardens. Pollution, however, was slowly becoming a problem due to coal fires and soap-boiling. Evelyn told how

> this horrid smoke obscures our churches and makes our palaces look old . . . . It fouls our clothes and corrupts the waters

46 Views of Cambridge from the east and from the west. Evelyn thought it was a "low, dirty, unpleasant" town.

▼

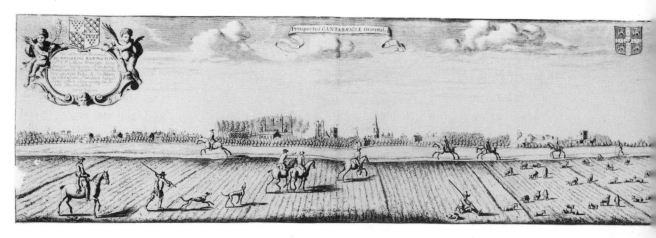

47 Heavy smoke is shown rising from the houses in this picture of London as early as 1616. Pollution was an increasing problem.

so that the very rain and refreshing dews that fall in several seasons precipitate this impure vapour, which with its black and tenacious quality, spots and contaminates whatsoever is exposed to it.

Towns were a strange mixture of old and new. Many medieval houses still stood, though not necessarily in good condition. Built higgledy-piggledy, they hung over the winding streets below and prevented fresh air and sunlight from filtering down. During the Commonwealth a tax was imposed on the building of new houses so that only the wealthy could afford to improve their living conditions. The streets were narrow, and because there was no efficient sanitation, they flowed over with all sorts of unhygienic rubbish.

London
London had a population of almost half a million, which was a large percentage of the entire population. It was overcrowded, noisy, insanitary, colourful and bursting with life. A visitor to London complained that the buildings were

as deformed as the minds and confusions of the people . . . for the magistrate has neither no power nor no care to make them build any uniformity, which renders it . . . a very ugly town, pestered with hackney coaches and insolent con-men, shops and taverns, noisy and such a cloud of sea coal as if there be Hell on Earth . . . . The persistent smoke . . . leaving a soot upon all things . . . and so fatally seizing upon the lungs of the inhabitants that the cough and consumption spare no man. I have been in a spacious church where I could not discern the minister for the smoke, nor hear him for the people barking.

Another visitor was rather more flattering:

> Building with brick has been very graceful to the City of London, and is very beneficial in preserving the same from fire; also for the preservation of timber, for the avoiding of the many juttings and encroachments on ground, the darkening of light, the straightening and stifling of the streets . . . and the infection of plague; the excessive breeding of vermin which occurs in wood houses.

The narrow, cobbled streets were supposed to be lit at night with torches and lanterns.

48 The style of building in Puritan times. This house in Norfolk was built in 1655.

49 London Bridge was crowded with houses in the seventeenth century.

The Thames was used effectively as an additional road, the river boats competing with the hackney carriages for passengers. In the winter the Thames often froze completely, and Frost Fairs were held on it. According to Fynes Moryson, London Bridge "numbered among the miracles of the World" and had nearly two hundred people living on it, as well as numerous shops and taverns. Here also on poles hung the heads of traitors — severe warning to all potential evil-doers. St Paul's was a popular meeting place and also contained "the general mint, of all famous lies, [where] all inventions are emptied . . . and not a few pockets".

Shops

London and every other town, no matter how small, were full of people trying to make a living by buying and selling. Street

50   Fleet Street, with its shops and taverns.

traders shouted their wares from every corner, and almost everything from clothes to kitchen utensils could be bought from street barrows. Shops were on the ground floors of buildings, and often had a workroom in the back. Potential buyers were free to walk in and look.

Most shopkeepers, such as bakers and millers, were given maximum and minimum prices which they were allowed to charge, and they were subjected to very strict trade rules. A baker was not allowed to give more than thirteen loaves in one dozen (hence the expression "a baker's dozen"), while butchers were not allowed to kill calves under five weeks old. The price of beer was fixed as no less than one penny a quart, but no more than ten shillings a barrel. Here are some typical prices for the year 1650:

1 quart wine (Spanish)	1s 6d (7½p)
1 quart wine (French)	7d (2½p)
1 chicken	6d (2½p)
1 rabbit	13s (65p)
1 ox	144s (£7.20)
Linen	1s 6d per sq. yard (7½p)
Shoes	24s (£1.20)
Bullets	£18 10d a ton (£18.04)
Tobacco	7s per lb (35p)
Cheese	4d per lb (1½p)

Taverns and ale-houses

Foreigners were amazed at the abundance of coffee houses and taverns in English towns. One startled Frenchman reported:

I assure you that they [Englishmen] drink their crowned cups roundly, straining healths through their smocks, dance after the fiddle, kiss freely and term it an honourable treat.

There cannot have been many Puritans around when he saw all that going on! Puritan disapproval of drinking does not seem to have stopped anyone from enjoying his ale. In 1650 there were seventy-four taverns and ale-houses in Fleet Street alone. Taverns were slightly higher class than ale-houses, and served food as well as ale. For a reasonable price, beef, mutton, cheeses, fish and pies could be purchased. Taverns were also pleasant places to enjoy a smoke:

If moderately and seasonably taken . . . [tobacco] is good for many things; it helps digestion, taken a while after meat; a leaf or two steeped over night in a little white wine is a vomit that never fails in its operations.

Ale-houses were closed on Sundays and fast days. Puritans made sure that every ale-house had a licence and only a certain number were allowed in each parish. In one month one third of all the ale-houses in Warwickshire were closed down. Puritans hoped that "sober people abhorred the multitude of ale-houses" and did not go into them anyway.

Coffee houses, chocolate and tea

The first coffee house in London opened in 1652, but Oxford claims to have had one as early as 1650. Coffee was introduced from Turkey and it was believed to help digestion, procure alacrity and strengthen the heart and brain. In 1657 the owner of

51 A London coffee house just after the Puritan period

52 A postboy with his large leather bag for ➤ letters.

the Rainbow Coffee House was up before the courts for "making and selling a drink called coffee, whereby making the same, he annoyeth his neighbours by evil smells".

Chocolate had been available since 1600, but the first shop opened in 1657. Chocolate cost between 10 and 15 shillings (50-75p) a pound and so only a few families

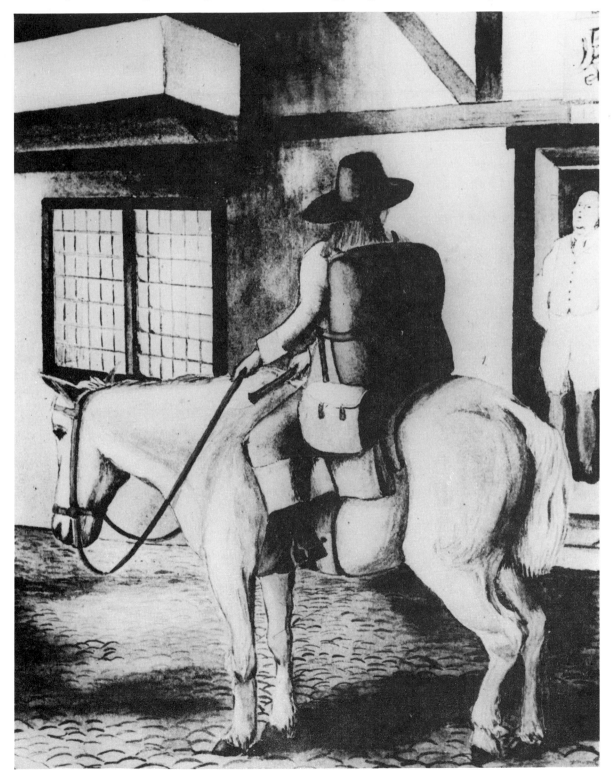

bothered to buy it. We would find it very different from today's hot chocolate, for it was drunk cold, without milk or sugar.

Tea was also introduced during Puritan times. In 1658 the following advertisement appeared:

> That excellent and by all Physicians approved China drink, called by the Chinese Tay, Tcha by other nations, alias Tea, is sold at the Sultaness Head, a Cophee house in Sweetings rents by the Royal Exchange, London.

Tea cost about £4 10s per pound. It was drunk without milk. Conscientious Puritan families cannot have used these new drinks, since they were all expensive luxuries.

The postal service

Private post, which had often been organized by inn-keepers, was abolished in 1656, and mail thereafter became the responsibility of the Government. All mail had to go through London, and so only people who lived in the capital or near one of the highways out of London could post letters. They had to take their letter to one of the postal offices, from which letters were despatched at the following prices: 2d (1p) for within an 80-mile radius of London; 3d (1½p) for letters to anywhere else in England or Wales; 4d (2p) to Scotland; and 6d (2½p) to Ireland. Prices were doubled if there was more than one sheet of correspondance. Post coaches left the Swan Inn in Holborn three times a week, their destinations including York, Salisbury, Plymouth, Edinburgh and Lancaster. The mail was carried in big leather bags, and the postman blew his horn every four miles to let people know he was coming. The coaches could not travel at much more than four miles per hour (6.4 kilometres) and so sending letters was a slow and also a precarious business, because of the state of the roads and the constant threat from highwaymen.

53 A pest house and plague pit. ➤

Health

Because there was no sanitation and no efficient health service, and because people lived in such crowded rooms, diseases spread rapidly with often devastating effects. There were pest houses where, at a charge of 2d (1p) a day, a person infected with plague could live in a special cabin, but once someone had this disease he was unlikely to survive very long. When someone died, "searchers", usually old women, searched the body and reported the cause of death to the parish clerk. Here is a typical list of reported deaths in London for the week 11-18 January 1650:

> of the plague 0; abortive 15; cough 2; drowned at St James Duke Place 1; grief 1; killed 28 (one by a fall of a piece of timber, in Tower Street, and 27 by the blast of gunpowder); impostume 1; palsy 1; Scurvy 1; smallpox 11; Surfiet 1; teeth 15; Lissicke 4; wind 2; vomiting 1.

Although medieval methods of medicine were still practised, much progress was being made and doctors were becoming an increasingly professional class.

Merchants

Merchants were becoming a prosperous class. It is estimated that there were 2,000 eminent merchants, 8,000 lesser merchants and 50,000 "shopkeepers" thriving in London during this period. London and other ports such as Bristol were flourishing trade centres and the homes of many merchant families. This poem about a merchant's wife, gives some idea of how wealthy the merchants were becoming:

> *Satin on solemn days, a chain of gold,*
> *A velvet hood, rich border and sometimes*
> *A dainty minever cap, a silver pin*
> *Headed with a pearl, worth 3d and thus far*

You were privileged, no-one envied it
It being for the City's honour that
There should be a distinction between
The wife of a patriarch and a plebeian.

Apprentices

At the age of about seven many boys were apprenticed to a master to learn a trade. An apprenticeship was seven years long, and the conditions concerning it were carefully laid down in the Statute of Artificers of 1563. An apprentice lived with his master, who fed and clothed him and taught him his craft. In return, the apprentice promised to be obedient and respectful. It seems that this promise was not always kept! Apprentices were lively and vocal, and even dared to go on strike as a protest against the Puritans for abolishing their holidays. Here is how one apprentice described his job:

I was to make clean the shoes, carry the ashes and dust, sweep the shop, cleanse the sink (and a long, nasty one it was), draw the beer, at washing times to fetch up coals and kettles.

It sounds as if he was doing the dirty work rather than learning any craft. If an apprentice dared to misbehave, or to write home complaining, as this one did, punishment was swift and severe:

No sooner was I come into my master's

57

house, but he seeing me, enters his closet, from whence he fetches a lusty balloon cane . . . and without by your leave, or with your leave, he takes me by the hand, and lifting up his sword arm like a fencer, he gives me a lusty thwack over the shoulders [and said] Sirrah, I'll teach you to run and make complaints to your father.

At the end of his apprenticeship the boy was expected to make a "masterpiece" — an item which would be judged by the "masters" of his craft, that is, the most skilled craftsmen. If this was successful, the apprentice became a qualified craftsman.

Fire

Fire was always a threat, as the many wooden buildings in towns needed only a tiny spark to set them all ablaze. This fire of 13 February 1655 must have been a typical occurrence:

a sad fire in Fleet Street, that had burnt down near 20 houses and half as many more were spoiled, from the Horn Tavern unto Fetter Lane. It began at Mr Gayne's, a grocer, by a great fire where they were drying sugar, in whose house was a

54   The German fire-engine which was invented ➤ in 1657.

barrel of gunpowder; one was spoiled with it, that fell from a ladder, another broke his arm, a woman bruised by a fall. The loss is very great.

There was no fire service, as we know it today, but every large town had syringes which held half a gallon of water, and were squirted onto the fire. The first fire-engine was invented in 1657 by a German, and consisted of a sledge with a water cistern on top, which when pumped, gushed out water.

Crime

Towns swarmed with every kind of criminal, from petty rogues and cut-purses, to swindlers and murderers. The Puritans introduced severe measures in an attempt to lessen the crime rate. An Act of 1657 stated that "all idle, loose and dissolute persons" were to be publicly whipped and then sent to a house of correction — in other words, someone could be punished just for looking lazy. Duelling was forbidden, and if someone was killed in a duel, it was treated as murder.

55   Puritans crowded to see the execution of the Earl of Strafford in 1641.
▼

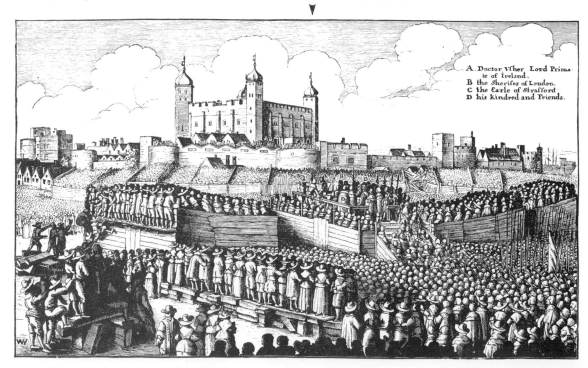

A. Doctor Vsher. Lord Primate of Ireland.
B the Sherifes of London.
C the Earle of Strafford.
D his kindred and friends.

As there was no efficient police force, it was difficult to enforce the law, but punishments and executions were common sights, and drew large crowds. For petty crimes, such as thieving or swearing, misbehavers were put in the stocks or the pillory, or were publicly whipped. Hanging was reserved for a multitude of crimes, not all of them serious by today's standards. Gibbets were erected at Smithfield, the Royal Exchange and Cheapside in London. Many other towns have a Gibbet Lane, recalling the site of hangings. On 10 May 1652 Evelyn made this rather sad entry in his diary: "I saw a miserable creature burning, who had murdered her husband."

Travel
Within towns, hackney carriages or private coaches were the most common means of transport, after a pair of feet.

The wheels of the London carts were very broad, and not plated with iron, because they would destroy the pavement. These carts are obliged to have a

56   A private coach of about 1650.

road conditions made coaches rarely punctual. On the road the greatest danger was from highwaymen. On 11 June 1652 Evelyn was accosted by two cut-throats who stole from him

> two rings, one an emerald with diamonds, the other an onyx, and a pair of buckles set with rubies and diamonds which were of value, and after all bound my hands behind me, and my feet, having before pulled off my boots; they then set me up against an oak, with most bloody threats to cut my throat if I offered to cry out.

He was eventually released two hours later by a couple of passers-by.

57   The famous highwayman "Mulled Sack" in action. He was hanged in 1656.

number, as well as the hackney coaches, that people may know them again if they have any complaint to make against the driver.

Drivers, like today's taxi men, expected handsome tips.

For longer journeys, stage coaches had been recently introduced and were becoming very popular. The coaches were brightly painted and inside were upholstered in velvet, though they cannot have been very comfortable. John Evelyn had a very low opinion of them and called them "Hell carts". By 1658 coaches were running to Salisbury, Plymouth, Wakefield, Exeter and Durham. The journey to Salisbury from London took two days, while Exeter to London was a four-day journey. However,

8 Living in the Country

The total population of Puritan England was about 4.5 million. The vast majority of the people lived in the countryside, earning a living from the land. Half the land was under cultivation, although there were still huge areas of fenland and downland. During the 1650s half a million acres of fenland were reclaimed, to the fury of the inhabitants who lost their fishing and fowling rights.

On the whole, however, everyday life in the country did not change drastically under Puritan rule, for the farming remained the same, as did the family's complete involvement in it. Rural society saw only a few changes, mostly at the top of the social ladder. The old gentry, many of whom had been Royalist or Catholic, had their estates confiscated and given to Parliamentarians, many of whom were not always aware of how country gentry were meant to behave. Beneath the gentry came the yeomen, well-to-do farmers, who owned their own land. Many of this class became Puritans. Below them were the husbandmen, who were also farmers but usually rented their land. The last group (apart from vagrants) were the labourers, who hired themselves out to nearby farms. A labourer's income was so low, between 8-10d (about 4p) a day, that all members of his family were expected to work in order to boost the family income. His wife and daughters spent long hours spinning, his sons helped him with jobs around the farm, while small

58 **Working in the fields with a simple plough was hard work.**

children looked after the animals or worked in the garden. Most families had a cottage garden and a few animals, such as a cow, pig or hens. Women, unless they were midwives or dairy-maids, did not earn more than 4d (1½p) a day, while children earned even less than that. Daunting as this life sounds, it appealed to Puritan families who thought that the harder they worked, the closer they got to Heaven.

Some things did change. Pastimes were banned and traditional country festivals were stopped and this left the people with little relief from continual hard work. The dull routine was slightly enlivened by visits to the weekly market, where mothers gossiped and children gazed longingly at the goods for sale. There were also pedlars who travelled from village to village and house to house, selling anything from kitchen utensils to pretty ribbons. An entry into an account book dated 1653 reads: "For tape, black ribbon and two fine ivory combs for the children from the pedlar 7s 0d [35p]''. However, such simple pleasures can hardly have compensated for the forbidden delights of a country Christmas or the dancing and revelry of Mayday.

Childrens' jobs
Children had to work just as hard as their parents and were expected to pull their weight from a very early age. Girls had to be skilled in an enormous variety of tasks, including spinning, candle-making, churning butter and mixing herbal remedies. Boys' jobs demanded more muscles. They spent their time hoeing, ploughing, sowing or

◄ **59 A Puritan Girl, by G. Boughton. The painting seems to suggest the dull life of the country girl of Puritan Times.**

60 Haymaking.
▼

helping with carpentry work. Small children were kept busy running errands, taking messages or acting as scarecrows. During harvest in August or September the whole family worked all day to get the crop in before the weather broke. It must have been back-breaking work. However, according to Dorothy Osborne, a lady who enjoyed travelling round the countryside, a rural life was a pleasant one:

> I walk out onto a common that lies hard by the house, where a great many young wenches keep sheep and cows, and sit in the shade singing ballads . . . . I talk to them and find they want nothing to make them the happiest people in the world.

Country homes

Yeomen lived in modest farmhouses with approximately eighty to one hundred acres of land. The houses had up to ten rooms, plus out-buildings such as the buttery, dairy, granary and sometimes even the kitchen. Most yeomen families could afford to have glass in their windows, and modern fireplaces with chimneys in the walls, instead of the open fire in the centre of the floor. Logs, dung and peat were the usual fuels, while candles and rushlights provided light. Furniture was sparse but sturdy, and had probably been handed down through the generations. Collapsible truckle beds with feather mattresses were the usual kind of bed, unless the family was wealthy enough to own a four-poster. Utensils were plentiful and varied, made out of wood, pewter or earthenware.

A labourer and his family lived in a tiny, two-roomed cottage, which, by law, was supposed to be surrounded by at least four acres of land. These houses were timber-framed, with wattle and daub walls (woven hazel twigs covered with mud and dung, then plastered over) and a thatched roof. Sometimes a labourer's home was little more than a hut, made out of mud and sticks. It must have been horribly dark, cramped and smokey inside, for there was no chimney, no glass and only the minimum of furniture. The main room of the labourer's house was called the hall and was the living area, while the second room, called the chamber, was used as a bedroom. Cooking was done either in the hall, over an open fire, or outside. Sometimes the house had a loft which was used for storage or as another bedroom. Beds were straw-filled pallets (like sacks) which were pulled out when needed.

Food

The quantity and quality of the food available to country families depended on the harvest, the size of the family and the time of year. If there had been a bad harvest, if the family had many mouths to feed, or if it was winter-time, then food was very short. A country diet consisted mainly of dark, rye bread, cheese, vegetables, meat, fish and ale. In the winter cheese was a substitute for fresh meat. Half the population had meat at least once a day, while the remainder ate it at least twice a week.

62   This country family appears to have ample meat to eat.

Yeomen seem to have done better: they

> shall have as many joints as dishes, no straggling joint of a sheep in the midst of a pasture of grass, beset with salads on every side, but solid substantial food.

Ale was drunk at every meal, in spite of Puritan disapproval. It cost about 1d (½p) per quart and was spiced, sweetened with honey, or diluted with water for children. Water and milk were thought to be suitable drinks only for children or the very old. Milk was usually made into butter or cheese.

Poor families

No meat, no drink, no lodging (but the floor)
No stool to sit, no lock upon the door,
No straw to make us litter at night
Nor any candlestick to hold the light.

This sums up the gloomy situation for an alarming number of poor families. The Elizabethan Poor Relief Act of 1601 had said that each parish was to take responsibility for its poor. Every parish therefore had an overseer whose job it was to make

sure that all poor families were looked after. Puritans, however, treated the poor harshly and urged people to be "strict at least in governing the Poor". They did not realize that unemployment was not voluntary, and thought that people were poor simply because they did not work hard enough. In other words, poverty was their own doing.

Poor people, including children, who refused to work for whatever reason, but who were physically able, were sent to houses of correction, where they were whipped. Begging was strictly forbidden, but it was difficult to enforce such a law. Pauper children were provided with work such as spinning or farming, while others were apprenticed to learn a useful trade. Some parishes built houses on waste land for their poor families.

The poor, like everyone else in the country, were expected to attend church on a Sunday. They were lured to church with the promise of alms if they attended regularly. But they had little choice about going, for if they did not turn up, they were fined or sent to a house of correction.

The poor who did manage to find jobs were worked almost to death. This passage shows how easy it was to become destitute, and how blameless the people were:

it is the custom of men nowadays . . . that they toil their servants while they can labour and consume their strength and spend them out; and then when age cometh and their bones are full of ache and pain . . . they turn them out of doors, poor and helpless . . . and they must either beg or starve . . . and thus it cometh to pass that many become thieves and vagrants.

For those unfortunate fathers who got into debt, the future was very bleak:

Tear forth the fathers of poor families
Out of their beds, and coffin them alive
In some kind clasping prison
where their bones
May be forth coming when the
flesh is rotten.

63   In the pillory.

64 A punishment for women was to duck them in the river.

Law and order

The countless vagrants and beggars wandering around the countryside made enforcing the law a continual problem. Every village had a constable: "the parish makes the constable and when the constable is made, he governs the parish." He had to prevent trespassing and poaching, look out for vagrants, make sure that taxes were paid, dispose of illegitimate children, prevent drunkenness from erupting in ale-houses and enforce all the Puritan measures. He also had to have the following qualities:

> *A constable must be honest and just*
> *Have knowledge and good report*
> *And able to strain with body and brain,*
> *Else he is not fitting for aught.*

The most common punishments he meted out, for petty offences such as drunkenness and brawling, were a spell in the stocks, the pillory or a quick ducking for wives. More serious misdemeanours were punishable by a visit to the house of correction or county gaol. Child offenders were whipped.

Date List

1603	James I came to the English throne
1604	Millenary Petition and Hampton Court Conference
1620	Pilgrim Fathers sailed to America
1625	Charles I came to the throne
1640	Maypoles ordered to be taken down
1641	Demands made for a northern university, with Durham being the eventual choice
1642	Start of the English Civil Wars
	All sports and amusements such as football and dancing banned
	First ordinance banning the theatre passed
1644	Christmas day made into a fast day, instead of one of celebration
1647	The celebration of Easter forbidden
1648	End of the Civil Wars
1649	Execution of Charles I
	Start of the Commonwealth or Interregnum
1650	Swearing made into an offence, punishable by fines
	First English music publisher in business
1652	First London coffee house opened
	Civil registration of births, deaths and marriages made compulsory
	Prayer Book replaced by the Puritan Directory
1653	Presbyterian system adopted in England
	Cromwell became Protector
1654	England captured Jamaica
1656	First English opera produced
	Private Post abolished and mail became the responsibility of the Government
1657	First chocolate shop opened in London
	First fire-engine invented
	Cromwell offered the crown, but refused and became Lord Protector instead
1658	Cromwell died
1660	Restoration of Charles II

Glossary

Baptists	a religious group which believed in the total immersion of the body at baptisms
Church Settlement	The Act of 1558 which laid down that Protestantism was the faith of England
ducking	a punishment for scolding wives and suspect witches: they were ducked into water on the end of a special chair
elder	an important and influential member of the Presbyterian church
Established Church	the Church of England, as established in 1558
Fifth Monarchy Men	a religious group which daily anticipated the second coming of Christ
frost fairs	fairs which were held on ice, when the Thames froze over in exceptionally cold winters
Independents	extreme Puritans who wanted a decentralized church with power in the hands of the congregations
Jacobean	the name given to the early Stuart period
Parliamentarian	someone who supported Parliament during the Civil Wars 1642-48
pillory	a wooden structure in which a person's head and arms were enclosed as a punishment
Presbyterians	a religious group who believed that there should be no Bishops, but government by the congregations and elders
Puritan Directory	this replaced the Prayer Book and outlined how services were to be directed
Quakers	a religious group who got their name by literally quaking with religious fervour
Royalist	someone who supported King Charles I during the Civil Wars
Sabbatarianism	the belief that Sunday should be a day of total rest, with no activity permitted except for the worship of God
Separatists	a religious group who wanted total separation from the Church of England
truckle bed	a bed which could be wheeled out when required

Books for Further Reading

Ashley, Maurice, *Life in Stuart England*, Batsford, 1962
Burton, E., *The Jacobean at Home*, Secker and Warburg, 1962
Colloms, B., *The Mayflower Pilgrims*, Wayland, 1973
Harrison, M. & Royston, O.M., *How they lived, 1485-1700*, Basil Blackwell, 1965
Quennell, M. and C.H.B., *A History of Everyday Things in England*, Vol. II, 1500-1799, Batsford, 1960
English Life in the Seventeenth Century, Pictorial Sources Series, Wayland

Index

The numbers in **bold type** refer to the figure numbers of the illustrations